You Need to Know

By Pat Lynn

Illustrated by Ashlee Maute

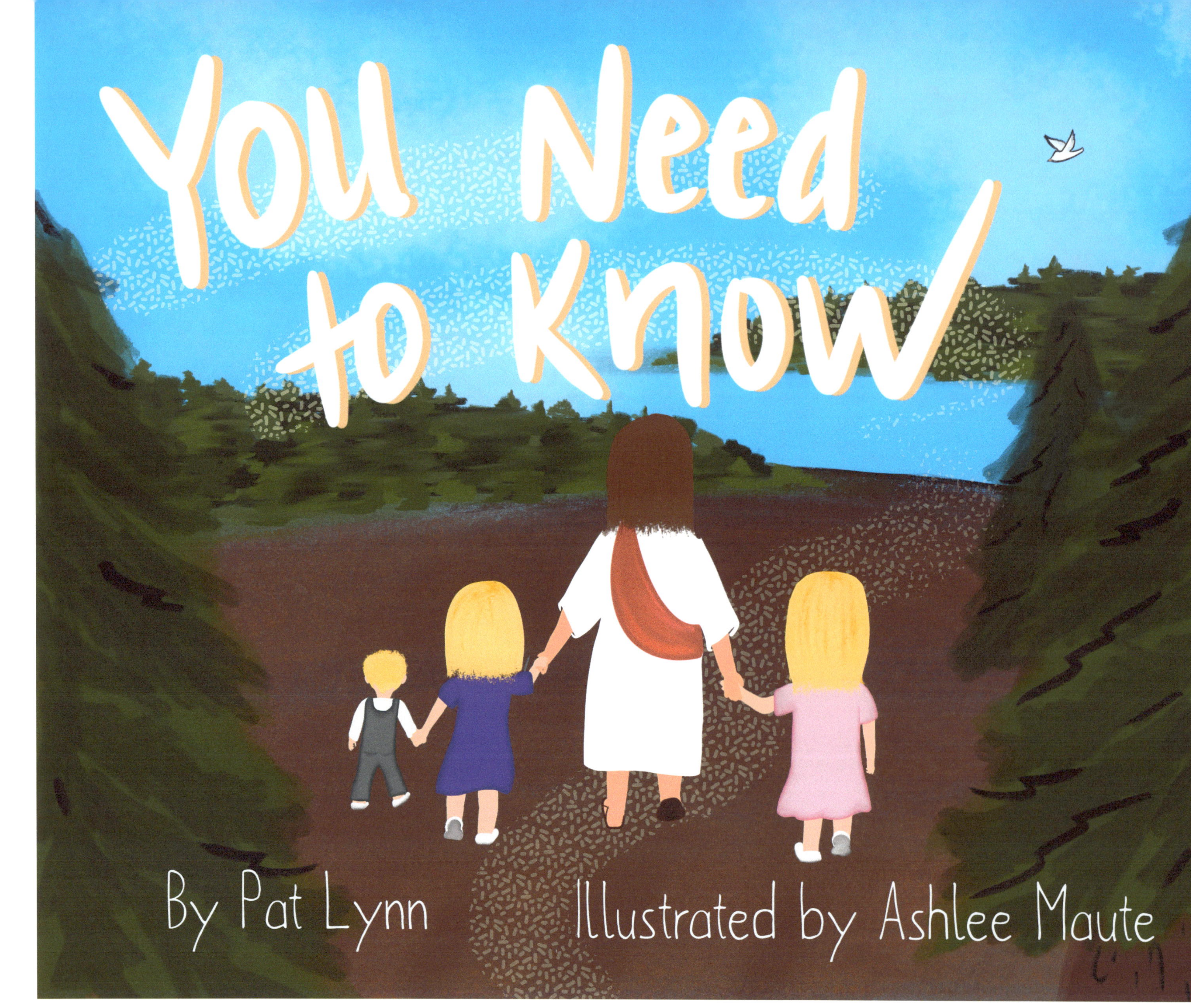

You Need to Know
By Pat Lynn
Illustrated by Ashlee Maute

"I knew you before I formed you in your mother's womb." - Jeremiah 1:5NLT

"For I know the plans I have for you," declares the Lord, "plans to prosper you and not to harm you, plans to give you hope and a future." - Jeremiah 29:11 NIV

"Do not conform to the pattern of this world, but be transformed by the renewing of your mind. Then you will be able to test and approve what God's will is — his good, pleasing and perfect will." - Romans 12:2NIV

This book is dedicated to my kids and to the truth that every child is made by God's incredible design, both on purpose and for a purpose.
\- Pat Lynn

Far beyond the bright city lights of Seattle,
and across the
Salish Sea...

...Across the great Hood Canal...

... Tucked into an old growth forest, just outside a little town called Sequim, lived a family with the last name of Lynn.
LYNN

There is Mr. and Mrs. Lynn, and their three children: Kennedy, Emma, and James. They also have two small fish, and a white fluffy dog named Oaken.

Everything at the Lynn home has a purpose. Mr. Lynn likes to say that God makes things "on purpose and for a purpose." And by His example, "so should we." For instance, the Lynn home has a ramp that reaches from the driveway to the front door.

Although it is used almost everyday as a bicycle ramp for Kennedy, Emma and James, it was built with a very specific and important purpose. The ramp makes it much easier for Mr. Lynn to reach the front door of the house with his walker.

Mrs. Lynn believes in purpose too.

She has organized her home so every space is used for good. There are spaces for learning, working, discovering and playing.

She also spends her work days helping others discover that they have purpose too.

Kennedy is a very confident six year old. She finds joy in singing and dancing and loves to use her imagination to invent games to play with her little sister.

Emma is an adventurous and inquisitive four year old. She is brave and kind. She loves to be a helper and watch over her baby brother James. Anything her big sister Kennedy can do, Emma believes she can do better.

James has just turned two.

He is kind hearted and adventurous. James loves dancing,
wrestling and playing with tractors.

Every night after dinner, Mrs. Lynn bathes her children, wrestles on their pajamas and helps them brush their teeth. Then, the family sits down in the living room to reflect on God's blessings and read a bedtime story.

One night, just before storytime, Kennedy, who is always full of questions, turned to her father and asked,

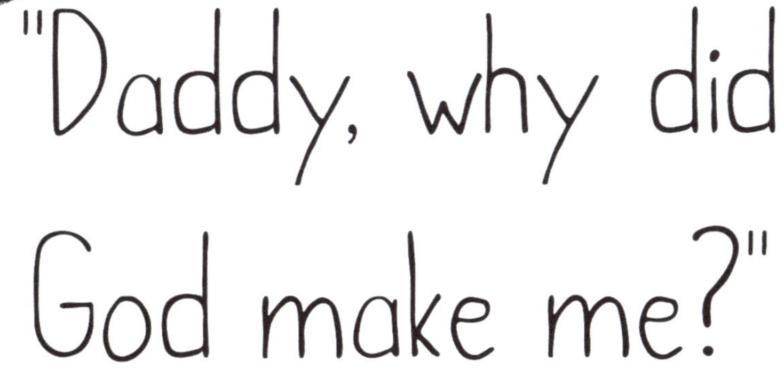

Mr. Lynn thought for a moment, then turned to his children and told them a truth that every child deserves to hear. He said:

You need to know that you were made by design.
From your fingers to your toes to the color of your eyes.
You need to know that you were made with great joy.
God knit you together in mommy's tummy with pride..

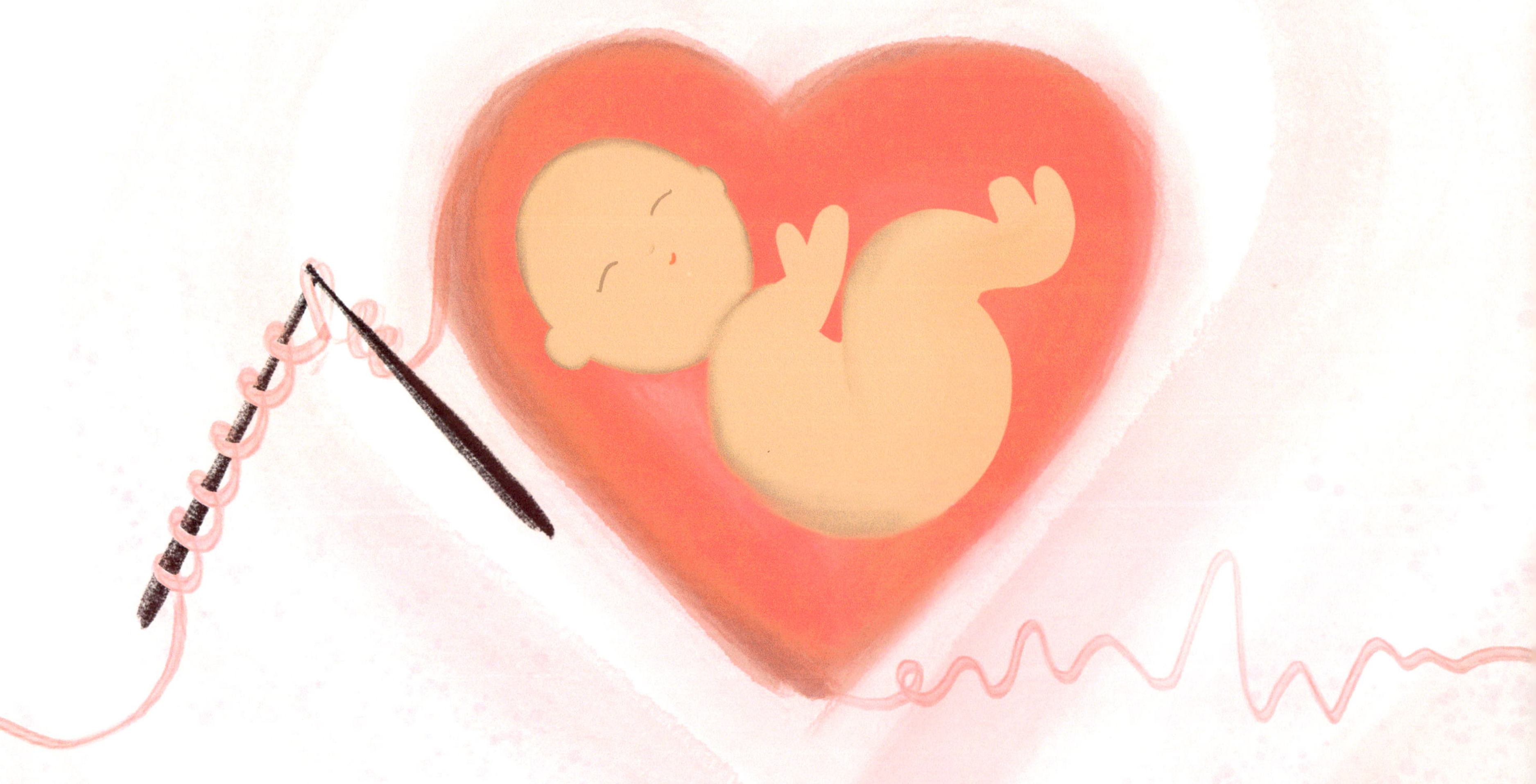

You need to know that your life was on purpose.
God knew you; he saw you before the Earth
had a surface.

You need to know that God loves you this way. He made you on purpose and he made you for play.

From your head to your toes and even your name, God made you on purpose, His love to display.

You need to know Jesus loves you, he does.
He loves you and knows you and watches from above.
God's Way
You need to know that God has plans for your life.
patience
joy
peace
kindness
goodness
faithfulness
Plans for running, playing and having such fun, and plans for bringing great joy to you and everyone.

You need to know
God made you a star. Not for
riches or fame but to shine His
light where you are.

You need to discover your
talents and gifts. God gave them
to you to use them for this.

You need to know the words you say matter,
so pick words that build up,
pick words that don't shatter.
TOY
HATE

You need to know that God loves you always. On good days and bad days, on happy and sad days. God loves you the same; He loves you always.

You need to know that God knows where you are! He's not surprised when you're near or you're far. He knows your heart; He sees it alive. God takes great joy in watching you thrive.

You need to know that God cares how you feel; when you're sad or you're angry or you're feeling alone. Jesus says not to worry; His Father is still on the throne.
You need to know God listens to prayers. He hears you and will help you so pray like you care.

You need to trust in God's plan for your life. He has one that's perfect; He has one that's right. You need to listen to the letters God left you. They're full of love; they're words that will direct you.
faith
hope

Jesus loves me this I know, for the Bible tells me so.
These are the words you need to remember. When the world tells you differently,
brush it off like a feather. Then stand up and walk it off;
Jesus loves you, remember.

With that, Mr. and Mrs. Lynn tucked their children in for the night. They prayed over them, and headed to bed knowing that God has His purpose for tomorrow too.

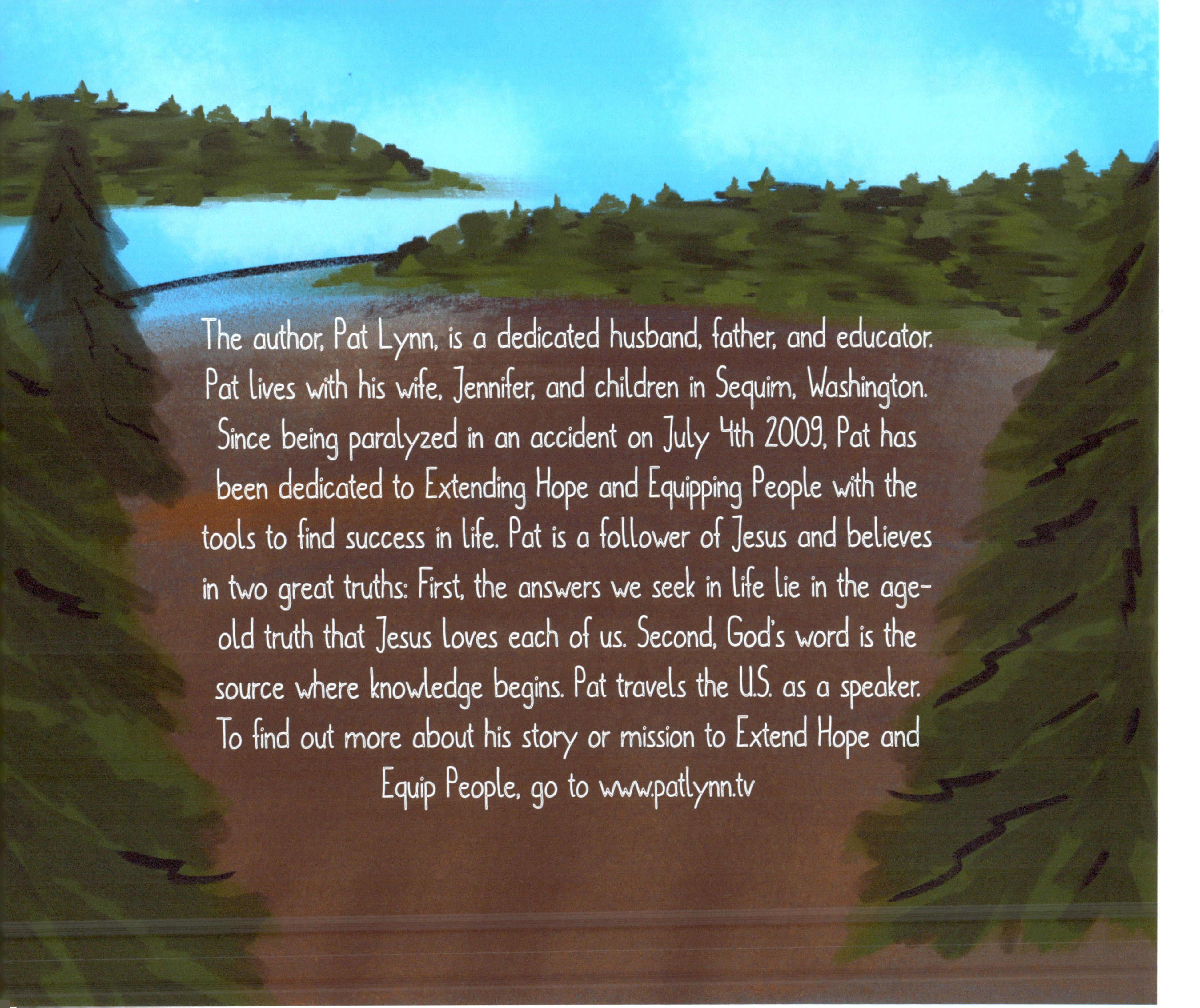

The author, Pat Lynn, is a dedicated husband, father, and educator.
Pat lives with his wife, Jennifer, and children in Sequim, Washington.
Since being paralyzed in an accident on July 4th 2009, Pat has
been dedicated to Extending Hope and Equipping People with the
tools to find success in life. Pat is a follower of Jesus and believes
in two great truths: First, the answers we seek in life lie in the age-
old truth that Jesus loves each of us. Second, God's word is the
source where knowledge begins. Pat travels the U.S. as a speaker.
To find out more about his story or mission to Extend Hope and
Equip People, go to www.patlynn.tv